"*What to Miss When* is hilarious and absolutely horrifying. If you think the quarantine habits you developed are unique and charming, read this book to be put in your place. But I beg of you, gift that to yourself, it'll make you feel less alone. 'I'm a feminist, I got the memo' is Stein's perfect disclaimer when shouting the things so many of us are afraid to even whisper. It's a specific kind of book that helps us remember how things were, that serves as a map for our children to understand why we are the way we are. This book is one of them."

—Olivia Gatwood, author of *Life of the Party*

"Early on in Leigh Stein's *What to Miss When*, the speaker says she 'must be some basic bitch to click / "Decameron and Chill?" in *Town and Country*,' and we know we're in for a ride through the pandemic that has some 'mischief' in it, which appropriately is the book's final word. It's this mischief, Stein's relentlessly refreshing humor about the 'new normal'—equal parts rueful self-deprecation and excoriating cultural critique—that makes this book such a worthy artifact of the American experience of the pandemic. As the speaker of these poems quits drinking, stress cleans, obsesses over social media, binge-watches television and movies, plans a wedding no one asks about anymore, and hits her goal weight 'without bringing Gloria Steinem into it,' we see a reflection of ourselves that's as hilarious as it is painful. This 'is America,' she says, 'where we livestream our freedom / to hurt and call it content,' where 'liberty means freedom to make choices / relative to your income bracket,' where 'we're starving for someone to blame / for our broken systems. We'd cancel a baby / if it gave us five seconds of relief.' She reveals how ironically masked we all are in this decadent culture that can't come to a consensus about the safety of literal masks, and as scathing as she is about all the 'white people / who spent the summer studying abroad / on Black Instagram learning to speak / privilege,' she turns the sharpest lens on herself, how her 'private self submits / anecdotes for [her] public / self's consideration,' how she regrets 'what [she] didn't mask / behind a better joke,' how she keeps touching the 'tiny slot machine' of her phone 'to see if this time [she's] won.' It's Stein's recognition of her own 'inessential hands' that makes us feel how essential this book is, the great care behind the critique."

—Jason Koo, founder and executive director
of Brooklyn Poets

Praise for Leigh Stein

"Highbrow brilliant." —*New York* magazine

"By showing us that it's possible to make something beautiful and funny out of our supposed follies, Stein rescues the present." —Poetry Foundation

"Leigh Stein's poems know how to laugh it off after a stunning tumble down a flight of stairs." —Rob MacDonald, editor of *Sixth Finch*

"A startlingly developed and fearless voice." —*The Rumpus*

"Intimate, urgent, and laugh-out-loud funny." —Joe Meno, author of *Hairstyles of the Damned*

"Cheeky self-assured prose." —*O, The Oprah Magazine*

Praise for *Self Care*

"Though the turmoil at the center of [the novel] is entertaining, its twist ending a clawed swipe at the irony of the scarcity myth—the zero-sum foundation of capitalism—it's not the thing that kept me reading. Instead, it was Stein's deft navigation of the shades of superficial feminism, the lexicon of start-up culture and the tone of a generation reckoning with how to be honest with itself." —*Los Angeles Times*

"Leigh Stein's latest novel is as decadent and brutal as a vampire facial. It's an exposé of feel-good feminism, an indictment of contemporary capitalism, and an absolute treat to read. This book will make you laugh, gasp, and vow to get off social media for good—and it'll understand when you can't help but log right back on." —Julia Phillips, National Book Award finalist for *Disappearing Earth*

"[A] darkly witty romp through corporate feminism." —*HuffPost*

"Leigh Stein's novel might just be the hit of adrenaline you need to delete your apps permanently—or at the very least, leap off your couch and do something better with your time." —*San Francisco Chronicle*

"*Self Care* proves Leigh Stein's status as a great 'demolition expert' (Kenneth Tynan's term for Bernard Shaw) of the influencer era." —*The New Republic*

"Stein's sharp writing separates her from the pack in this exquisite, Machiavellian morality tale about the ethics of looking out for oneself." —*Publishers Weekly* (starred review)

"Just try not to snort your Moon Juice out your nose while laughing your ass off." —*Refinery29*

"A brutal dissection of 'Insta-worthy' culture, the unconscionable capitalistic impulses behind wellness ventures, and the farce of forced community building." —*Vulture*

"Brutal and brutally funny . . . Stein presents a punchy, bracing criticism of modern feminism's transformation into a commercialized hellscape of goat yoga, healing crystals, and 'girl bosses.'" —*Esquire*

"Merciless and mordantly funny . . . Stein gives her ruthless romp through influencer culture an authenticity born from a genuine love of the internet . . . This is the self-aware callout culture novel that we need, but don't deserve. Don't sleep on *Self Care* (unless your Fitbit tells you to sleep more—then do that, hydrate, and add 20 minutes of Headspace before reading)."   —*Salon*

"A novel of manners for our 280-character era."   —*Elle*

"Stein offers a look into the dark underbelly of these easily marketable spaces, the promise that a room full of women equals safety, and the egos and violence that sadly so often exist within them."   —*Bitch*

"*Self Care* is the bitchy beach read for people who wear a 'Bitches Get Shit Done' T-shirt, but who are also well-versed in debates about reclaiming the word 'bitch.' Stein is the kind of writer who would be at home both in *The New Yorker* and on a Tumblr page devoted to writing poems about *The Bachelor* . . . At its core, it's a very clever satire."   —*The A.V. Club*

"*Self Care* is a skewering mockumentary about influencer culture, internet feminism, and the infinite ways that big tech capitalizes on our worst fears and insecurities. Utterly teeming with humor, this is exactly the sort of book that

Dorothy Parker would have written if she'd been reincarnated as an Instagram celebrity." —Catherine Lacey, author of *The Answers* and *Certain American States: Stories*

"[A] hyper-timely—and unexpectedly heartfelt—satire of #girlboss culture and the wellness industrial complex . . . Compulsively readable . . . Brilliant." —*Kirkus Reviews*

"Wickedly talented Leigh Stein—for my money, one of our sharpest millennial writers—knows the internet, and she's used that intimate knowledge to write a pitch-perfect novel for our times. *Self Care* is a hilarious and sneakily moving send-up of what it means to try and live when every move you make is observed and dissected online, by a writer who sees the truth and says it with so much humor and heart you'll laugh (and maybe cry) out loud." —Julie Buntin, author of *Marlena*

"A titillating satire about our quest for validation and the lengths that some will go to for #selfactualization, *Self Care* is an intelligent, delightful read that will make your mind (and epidermis!) glow." —Courtney Maum, author of *Touch* and *Costalegre*

"Timely and playful . . . Offering a juicy glimpse into the pathos and ethos of the wellness industry and the influencers who make it all appear so shiny and bright."   —*Booklist*

"A smart critique of the wellness industry . . . but also a very fun read."   —*Betches*

"It's not just that I found *Self Care* wildly entertaining, I found it deeply illuminating. So this is how the clickbait gets cooked up! I learned, I laughed, I loved every page. What I especially admired was Stein's rare ability to be hilariously wicked while remaining deeply empathetic. I say skip your next juice cleanse and read this brilliant and delightful novel."   —Meghan Daum, author of
The Problem with Everything:
My Journey Through the New Culture Wars

WHAT TO MISS WHEN

ALSO BY LEIGH STEIN

The Fallback Plan
Dispatch from the Future
Land of Enchantment
Self Care

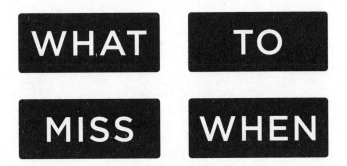

Poems

LEIGH STEIN

SOFT SKULL

NEW YORK

First Soft Skull edition: 2021

Library of Congress Cataloging-in-Publication Data
Names: Stein, Leigh, 1984– author.
Title: What to miss when : poems / Leigh Stein.
Description: First Soft Skull edition. | New York :
Soft Skull, 2021. |
Includes bibliographical references.
Identifiers: LCCN 2020047790 | ISBN 9781593766979 (trade
paperback) | ISBN 9781593766986 (ebook)
Subjects: LCGFT: Poetry.
Classification: LCC PS3619.T465 W48 2021 |
DDC 811/.6—dc23
LC record available at https://lccn.loc.gov/2020047790

Cover design & Soft Skull art direction by www.houseofthought.io
Book design by Wah-Ming Chang

Published by Soft Skull Press
1140 Broadway, Suite 704
New York, NY 10001
www.softskull.com

Printed in the United States of America
1 3 5 7 9 10 8 6 4 2

for Brian

Forget your life.

Okay I have.

—JENNIFER DENROW,
"California"

CONTENTS

WHAT TO MISS WHEN

THINK STARLIGHT

Think containment. Think caseload. Think
of your parents. Think of Lily, who taught you
the etymology of *stanza*—
a kind of stopping place, the room
where we self-quarantine. Think
of all the faces you've known by hand,
the curve of your lover's skull, how no one
ever admits they wish they'd worried more,
so you keep your panic on you at all times
like a passport. The paper reports the nameless
score, tally marks on the wall of a white stanza
where women in green speak a language
you don't understand and decide who deserves
the breathing machine. Think starlight:
it took so long to touch us,
we trusted we were spared.

PLAGUE AS LITERARY MOTIF

Spent all morning at my bookshelf searching
for something by someone who survived this.

I must be some basic bitch to click
"Decameron and Chill?" in *Town & Country.*

My first instinct is now *find out the death count*:
Boccaccio says 100,000. He names seven women

who were like, Even if we stop going to church,
we're still going to see the sick in the streets;

we're still going to hear all that dolorous wailing;
our dead servants' ghosts are mad infectious.

Yo, what wait we for? What dream we of?
At a villa outside Florence (click for slideshow),

the girls spend a fortune on lashes and a fortnight
drinking red wine from copper glasses,

confessing malaise in sexy baby voices to pass the time
while three hot guys weep openly—not 'cause of plague,

but 'cause they don't think anyone can see them
in their pods. This ten-day event poses the question:

Is love truly blind? The members of the *brigata*
slow-dance on their balconies and sing "Volare":

Let's fly. Once we accept futility
and the absurd as our new normal,

Jacques Barzun says that is when
we know decadence has set in.

PLAGUE DOCTOR COSTUME

Already I can't imagine what my life was like
three weeks ago. I'm homeschooling

my gel manicure, teaching her to tell me
the time, ordering perfume online

to spritz inside the beak of my mask,
a flirty bouquet to take the edge off

the plague. For three minutes,
we collectively mourned

the death of Kathy Griffin's mother. *RIP*
may your box of wine be full always.

Then we moved on to more urgent needs:
our own. Someone with more followers than me

said, *Remember when we were all going to stop*
drinking (haha) and bitch I did

nineteen days ago. Listen, I don't think
we should call women bitches either,

but I took the high road for three years
and the oxygen is too thin to breathe

up there. I'm wearing a fascinator
to my Zoom calls so no one knows

I'm sober. I'm listening to the same music
I played the last time I severed all connections,

moved to the desert, and lived in isolation with a man
who made me feel I'd arrived at the end of the world.

A PRACTICAL WEDDING

No one asks about my wedding dress anymore—
we don't know yet which version of the simulation
we're in. Watch me sew a mermaid gown

out of Clorox wipes on my YouTube channel,
Death Cab for Couture, and then decoupage
old plague tracts that say FLEE WIKKYD HEIRES

on my bathroom walls while my fiancé sleeps
off his bad humors. Budget-friendly decor tips
have never been a national emergency before;

witness the home organization influencers pivot
to hoarding #inspo. If this goes on much longer,
I'll have to learn how to do an updo. My dreams

about breaking my engagement ring
now happen in a rustic-chic reception hall,
where a string quartet plays "Fast as You Can"

but all the white Chiavari chairs are empty.
Inconceivable to hora solo, even on TikTok.
A hora needs a circle for transmission,

from the Greek *khoros*—those actors
assigned to tragedy, narrating
what the audience already fears to be true.

If we don't save the date, who will? In lockdown,
an author eating broccoli in her old gown
and veil gets ten thousand retweets. Am I crying

from envy or grief? My colors are hospital green
and blush pink, art deco meets influenza,
a custom chuppah canopy woven out of masks.

PARASITE (2019)

When I confessed my crush on Cuomo,
my patron said she knows him—or at least
she knows a guy who knows a guy
who can get her the last ventilator
when things fall apart. The closer
she got to the Kennedys, the more
I disassociated, picturing the Kim family
hiding in plain sight while the Parks
jerk each other off in silk pajamas.

I comfort one patron who can't escape
to her second home; I soothe another
whose passive income stream has run dry.
Here in the *banjiha* of my mind,
survival becomes a scheme, a stratagem
for when the shelves are empty
and the market betrays the citizens.
Meanwhile, in the glass house, riot fears
are keeping the upper class company.

UNCANNY VALLEY OF THE LADIES (1348)

I don't know about you, but all my staff
is basically dead, Pampinea tells the girls
she meets at the funeral. All I have left
is one maid and I'm frickin' scared.
If Fortune favored my birth
to noble boomers
with a château collection,
shall I not spend that Fortune
on you ladies, whom I have only just met?
We can live in one *locus amoenus*
today and another tomorrow;
our distress will be lessened
if for ten days we take turns
playing queen and bingeing
prestige TV because we're smarter
than the losers drinking themselves
to death in Florence. I've never seen
The Sopranos, Elissa says. Me neither,
says Lauretta. Everyone seems really into

the idea of fleeing the plague except
Filomena, who says, Dearest ladies,
it has been my experience
that when you put women together
in a dormitory or, say, an online yarn
community, they tend to destroy one another
psychologically, while disguising themselves
as nuns. Maybe we need some men
to role-play kings, seeing as Italy
is still a patriarchal society,
Elissa says, but all the men I know
are covered in boils. Lo and behold,
who should enter the church
but three young studs
who wouldn't mind rewatching
The Sopranos. I don't know
what you intend to do with your troubles,
Dioneo says, but I'm leaving mine
outside the gates of our afflicted city,
and just like that they're *innamorata,*
a merry company on their way
to villa numero uno, for the finest
wines, followed by a dance
that allows their hands to touch.

The young lovers tell their servants
to turn off all notifications
so they won't be disturbed
by news from the world beyond.

You be the nurse getting off
her twelve-hour shift;

I'll be the billionaire playboy
with a helicopter and a high libido.

Forget public transportation
when I've got you, babe.

I'll watch you shower like it's my job,
then transfer so much money into your account

you never have to put your uniform back on.
We can play ICU right here, in the hammock.

*

How can I let him touch my face
when I'm wearing all these serums?

Inner monologue from the front lines
of the year after the year after the year

that skincare became our collective
coping mechanism. *If I get smaller pores*

out of this, it will have been worth it.
Require kissing below the clavicle

as you flash back to the vulva episode
of *Goop Lab,* the first time a nonagenarian

has entered a fantasy—the Strega Nona of climax
there to reassure you you're rock-and-rolling right.

◆

Text the hottest ex you ever had.
Does he live and work on an organic farm?

Perfect. It's unlawful to get back together,
so the pulsing ellipsis of his reply

equals foreplay. Wave your Magic Wand
over the top of your sweatpants

for safety. If reluctance turns you on,
carpe diem. Imagine an intruder

who turns out to be him. You're not allowed to cum
until you've sung "Happy Birthday" twice.

LET'S BEAUTY TOGETHER

The chemical burn on my forehead
comes courtesy of the efficacious
skincare routine I began in quarantine,
hoping to look hotter than my nemesis
when we're seated side by side
at the reunion show. Customer service
says to keep using marula oil
and stop giving my golden retriever
red wine to distract the audience
from how often I refill my glass.
Mark thinks I'm afraid of commitment,
but I always follow through
on my worst instincts. In the mirror,
I apply glycolic acid to the only face
I'm allowed to touch. I'm exfoliating
until someone asks me
what's really wrong.

INCURABLE CHATTERBOX

> Years seem to have passed between
> Sunday and now.
> —ANNE FRANK, July 8, 1942

My oeuvre of sixteen thousand tweets
now reads like Anne's diary before hiding:

my weak marks in algebra, my crush calling
on the phone, the last of the fancy biscuits,

fascism as backdrop for my juvenilia.
Before the state of emergency,

we thought we could virtue signal
our way to the top of the list

Who's Spared. While you squabble
over who's paying their housekeeper

most generously, a call-up notice comes
for Anne's father and she pictures "lonely cells"

in concentration camps—she has no idea
what to actually fear. We do.

I'm in hiding with a man whose grandmother
saw Hitler on a trolley, fled to England,

survived the Blitz, outlived Anne by decades.
I'm papering my walls with Hollywood postcards,

not giving up on imagination or glamour
while I wait for my period to come

so I can finally stop crying. How long
until I'm forced to cut my beloved's hair?

When he begs to journey to CVS
for superior scissors, I try to scare him

with what I heard on our contraband radio:
a doctor tried to bring a thirty-eight-year-old,

who looked like her fiancé, back to life. She failed.
I confess my childhood fantasy was to live

like Anne: ration diet of endive, romance
with the sky, built-in End Times boyfriend.

She spent 761 days inside the house behind.
She would have loved how much we love her.

CATASTROPHE TOURISM

For my thirty days, Brian gave me a euro
from a vacation we took back in the B.C.
and we had spaghetti with the news
that the little Cuomo has corona.
Brian thinks running out of donuts
means a shopping expedition;
I said, Remember your grandmother
survived the Blitz with zilch.
Pretending this is a war
makes personal sacrifice possible.
(Didn't it seem unbelievable in *Jojo Rabbit*
how much wine flowed for ScarJo?)
Since I can't drink to celebrate,
I read a travel essay about Chernobyl—
the writer feels guilty for wanting to see
"what the end of the world looked like";
he's uncomfortable paying a man named Igor
to show him Pripyat's abandoned amusement
park. "I have three children. No mutants,"
says Igor. (How I wish I could read

an American travelogue by Igor:
see how dumb and graceless
we seem when we speak Ukrainian.)
The word *uncanny* appears four times,
surely not involuntarily, but Freud
would say it's the difference between
a single coat-check ticket that says 62
and seeing that number several times
in one day, including in your cruise ship
cabin. The uncanny is the familiar
made frightening: a field hospital
in Central Park instead of Fashion Week,
conspiracy theories about the governor's
nipple piercings. One summer,
Brian and I visited a Czech fortress
the Nazis turned into a transit camp
that became the setting of a hoax
to show how well the Jews were treated
in this "spa town" of intellectuals and artists,
poets and composers. Before the Red Cross
visited in 1944, they planted gardens,
painted houses, rehearsed their lines,
and even the children performed an opera
about outsmarting an evil organ grinder.

You won't believe what happened next
to the children, but it's true. In lieu
of a souvenir, I've kept one uncanny
image of our summer vacation: outside
the Nazi café, we ate ice cream.

STOCKPILE

Many of us suspected we might die one day,
but the grocery store risk adds a new twist.

Thích Nhất Hạnh would tell us
to observe our breath, in and out,

mindfulness a peaceful reminder
there still aren't enough masks.

Anyone who sees my list (turmeric,
quinoa, tofu) will call me Karen

and ask why I'm not staying home
so Americans on food stamps can shop

for the first ten days of the month,
unless you're in Texas, where

the right to religious freedom
trumps the rate of infection—

if you're in Texas, stock up
before the believers spread

the virus like an Easter egg hunt
in the aisles of Trader Joe's.

I, too, would rather have God
tell me what to do than the Twitter

scolds, whose compassionate hearts
are as big as Jared Kushner's.

Yes, the groceries exist.
No, they're not for you.

There were two packages of tofu
left, and I only took one—look

at me virtue signaling in my own poem.
Even without religion, we want to be counted

among the Good People who sweep
the supermarket ethically, buying

only the boxed rotini we need, hoping
God's son-in-law notices and saves us.

THRIVE

In my refurbished Airstream,
I wear the same sustainable
bamboo jersey knit romper

whether I'm in vashistasana
or putting my succulents in hospice.
I have discourse hypersensitivity,

so I had to sign off and now
I rescue another cockatoo
anytime I need distraction.

As long as my breasts stay
like this, my lover will handle
all the documentary footage

of our tiny-house lifestyle.
He's poly-curious, but
I get it. Sometimes I miss carbs

and then I come back to my "why."
If I had to be online all day,
I wouldn't have time to spiral

all the zoodles my fans need
to thrive. Being a mom is hard,
I get that, so why have kids?

I think of my pioneer ancestors,
how they would have loved
a passive income stream,

hormonal birth control, the opportunity
to have met me. When I'm ready
for my nervous breakdown,

it will be on my terms; this is America,
where we livestream our freedom
to hurt and call it content.

OUTSIDE TIME

I don't have anything to say about trees.
If you want trees, call Greta or the ghost
of Mary Oliver. An ongoing theme
in my work is readers accusing me
of writing books that won't be relevant
in the future—I want to live in that timeline,
too, where the influencers bore us so much
we stop paying attention and they go back
to trading their finite time on earth
for wages. Is Walt Whitman irrelevant
because his opium-eater, his lunatic,
and his quadroon girl make undergrads
uncomfortable? Back in the outside time,
fourteen-year-old Emily Dickinson pressed
flowers: jasmine for passion, a privet hedge
for privacy. Then she went inside basically
forever. Why are her poems universal,
not of a specific time and place?
She wrote about grief while living through
the Civil War. She was played by Molly Shannon
in a film re: her sexual appetite for her sister-in-law,

Sue. Do Emily's clandestine orgasms
not resonate with today's readers, who
have so much access to online porn?
The narcissism of small differences
is my universal theme. Outside, I walk
my routine loop through the landscaped
cul-de-sac, which is French for "road
to nowhere," observing all the flowering trees
that aren't verbal enough to reveal their names.
When I read that Sue put two heliotropes
in Emily's hands upon her death, I thought,
What a beautiful word, "to turn toward the sun"
in Greek. Like Emily, I prefer inside over out,
to sit in the same white dress, working overtime
on something that might touch the interior
of my beloved's mind—yours.

TIGER KING (2020)

I sometimes find President Trump's
voice reassuring. Not what he says.
Not the actual words . . .

—LORRIE MOORE

The caged tigers are hungry for whatever you have:
Walmart meat past its expiration date, a sickly calf,
short story master Lorrie Moore. She was asking for it

when she confessed his voice soothes her
like she's his pet. The caged tigers don't care
about your contributions to arts & letters,

that you sit in a distinguished chair you built
on the grounds of your personal exotic animal park—
they just want to eat. It's been weeks

since anyone threw a juicy thoughtcrime
into their pen. One of the older tigers,
who's been too busy birthing cubs

to keep up with her *New Yorker* subscription,
might need a younger tiger to explain
how we're starving for someone to blame

for our broken systems. We'd cancel a baby
if it gave us five seconds of relief. In one story,
Lorrie Moore offers a cure for depression:

stop drinking, stop smoking, stop eating sugar,
cut out caffeine. "Do this for three days," she writes,
"then start everything back up again. *Bam.*"

STRESS CLEANING

Since I'm not drinking, I turn myself on
by watching the gif of Mr. Clean
mopping the floor. I have thirty attachments
for my vacuum cleaner, and I know
which one to use for the silverware drawer
and which one to use when I notice
I'm having that nagging fear of death
again. At Costco, I bought a twelve-pack
of Magic Erasers, a recommended
substitution for sage burning
if you're one of those suburban white women
voters they're always talking about on TV.
I won't deny how many floral thong leotards
I own; they go with the bike shorts I wear
to my aerobics revival movement
meetups. Traveling back in time
always helps me break a sweat—
as does wiping down the baseboards,
pulling hair from the shower drain,

playing the martyr, getting high
on being the only woman I know
who cleans her own home.

SAFE (1995)

Woman goes to the doctor with shortness of breath
and vomit on her silk tea dress and you'll believe
what happens next: he asks her if she's *under a lot
of stress*. Woman says *yes*. Woman goes on fruit diet,
dodges humping with heartless husband, asks the help
for a second glass of milk, grapevines at aerobics
but can't break a sweat. Other women are jealous
of our woman, her porcelain skin and vulnerable
shoulder blades as she stalks her own property
at night, in the spotlight of the private security
patrol. The fumes of the San Fernando Valley
are killing her, along with the pressures
of polite society: get a perm, wear a peplum,
perform femininity by claiming you cannot control
yourself around ice cream cake. In the desert,
she tells a woman who's just as sick as she is
that her childhood bedroom had yellow
wallpaper. Remember how that story ends?
Her guru helped himself by plucking the lesions
from his skin like black pansies in a dream.

He can cure our woman, too, but only
if she admits she doesn't need the oxygen,
that the blooming sore on her forehead
is a symbol of her unwillingness to heal.

MY THERAPIST GAVE ME PERMISSION TO WANT TO LOSE WEIGHT WITHOUT BRINGING GLORIA STEINEM INTO IT

I hit my goal weight during the pandemic,
not because I got sick or was too anxious
to eat, but because I've been counting
every clementine since December
using an app they advertise on the subway
alongside poetry I was too cynical
to ever appreciate. I'm a feminist,
I got the memo: I'm not allowed
to post how much weight I lost, or
even that I *wanted* to cut back
on drinking every night
until I no longer felt guilty
about what I was doing
to shut up the first shift worker
who thought she could just tell
second-shift me what to do.
The evening crew works on different
problem sets, she should know that.

I tried leaving a Post-it on her desk,
Body positivity, ever heard of it?
I'm supposed to love the body I have
now, not the one I had six years ago,
before my J-O-B became drinking to get through
all the Facebook messages from women
telling on one another for not censoring their thoughts
enough for the sake of the community. Sick,
I know, how much I tried to pleasure the impossible-
to-please, like the Nobel Peace Prize was mine
if I could just figure out how to end the internecine
warfare of freelance feminists. Another glass
of Chenin Blanc got me closer to solving for *x*.
The third shift was when I used to lie in the dark
on the couch, scrolling for anything to distract me
from my ugly déjà vu. Now my body is a woman I
    remember;
we both clicked *yes* to accept the new terms of service.

AMERICAN HISTORY

A white woman outside a Baskin-Robbins holds
a GIVE ME LIBERTY OR GIVE ME DEATH sign,
kudos to Patrick Henry for inciting that other revolution—
King George on the Stop & Shop intercom
wasn't gonna tell *him* the grocery aisles were one-way now,
that's tyranny. Henry didn't want to be a slave to England,
but I wonder whether he would have provided masks
to the sixty-seven men and women who worked his property,
I'm sorry, who *were* his property. (He felt guilty. He might have.)
In America, liberty means freedom to make choices
relative to your income bracket. There's no prohibition
against thrill-seekers protesting the proposition
of "public health." Imagine if the woman's sign
had said MY BODY, MY CHOICE,
how we would have marched alongside her,
defended her against the haters, distributed
the weight of the fury by taking turns
when our arms grew tired. Instead
we make her into a meme, a Karen:
a woman who hasn't learned
how to correctly aim her rage.

ARE YOU GOING TO FINISH THAT?

What do you recommend?
Have you tried it before?
Which region of Italy is it from?
Can you tell me more about this one:
"full-bodied, black fruit, I'm so tired"?
Is the flavor profile more like the women
I never spoke to again or the women
who never again spoke to me?
What goes best with swordfish?
What goes best with sanctimoniousness?
What goes best with avoiding
thinking about what I have to do
tomorrow? Should we just split a bottle?
Is it too early to start? Did we ever figure out
why this night is the same as all others?
Are you going to tell your boss you quit?
Should we order another round?
Is it my turn to complain? Can someone please
explain why they unoaked the Chardonnay?
Why are you crying? Did you get enough to eat?

Do you ever wonder how we got to treat
ourselves this way? Or which of us will be the first
to leave the last sip in the glass?

WHAT TO MISS WHEN

I'm making an editorial calendar for my nostalgia.
Mondays are for attractions I once complained
about, the slow-motion crush of tourists, myself
among them. So everyone likes the French
Impressionists the most, so what? On Tuesdays,
I try to remember the orange blossom
scent of my sister's hair. On Wednesdays
I rank everything I've ever eaten
on an airplane. Thursdays are free
for missing red velvet seats,
the string section tuning to A,
a cough so minor it can be quieted
with a candy, standing ovations.
Touch I've saved for Fridays,
so I can spend all weekend
scrolling through my catalog
of *who, how, where, when.*

THE SECOND COMING

I've been keeping a bottle of red wine
for when "things fall apart," thinking
I'll know what the blood-dimmed tide
is loosed looks like when I see it.
As Joan Didion says, "Life changes fast."
One day you're a small business owner
in Berlin, the next thing you know
your children aren't allowed
to go to school. What rough beast
is calling the shots to make the stock
market outperform all reason?
When Yeats calls anarchy "mere,"
it's not trivial; he means *pure*,
undiluted chaos, what we on team blue
predict for team red if they reopen
their beaches, as if we're immune
to summer's charms, salt and sand,
slouching our pale shoulders towards
whoever has the sunscreen, for a moment
forgetting the second coming is at hand.

WHAT HAPPENS IF YOU CLICK IT

Did it work? Is it bigger?
Does it ask for a password?
Does it say which account
the money was deposited in?
What if you double click?
Did you check your spam?
Did you try closing all your tabs?
Did you send an inspirational quote
to the person in position #1?
Is the Wi-Fi working for you?
You don't have two-factor turned on?
What if you hold down the shift key,
take a screenshot,
say the pledge of allegiance,
change your underwear,
see if they offer free shipping,
check your heart rate monitor,
accept the cookies,
turn it off and back on again?
Is it working now?

THE NIEMÖLLER EFFECT

First they offered me a branded podcast
and I did not speak out—because
my process is really visual and people
need to see that. Then they came
and offered me my own glazed
dinnerware collection in ecru
and modern flatware in brushed gold
and resin that was actually kinda cute
but still I did not speak out because
who is throwing dinner parties right now?
No one. Then they came for my social media,
said fine, just be yourself, but only
the self that is likable, be *nice* for godsake,
and think of something tragic from your past
to disclose in your next recipe,
confessional seared scallops with broccoli rabe,
so we can turn the sympathy spotlight back
in my direction, just a girl at home chopping
onions through her tears, going viral
before they come for all the content farmers
and there's no one left to speak out for me.

BACK TO THE FUTURE (1985)

In 1955, everyone thinks Marty McFly
is wearing a life jacket, and they're not wrong:
if he fails to make his parents fall in love,
he'll never learn to swim. I had forgotten
the Oedipal plot, Marty psyching himself up
to get handsy with Mom so his dad can come
rescue the future, but it's Biff, that dick
who won't take no for an answer,
who opens the car door, easily cleaving
the story into its villains and heroes,
the men who use violence against women
and the men who use violence to stop
those men. O gods were it possible
for me to rewatch this movie like a man
and take a nostalgic drug trip on the wings
of a theme song, instead of filtering
everything I see through my lived experience
as Lorraine, topping off the vodka in her glass.
How much did she drink the night Marty
spent a week in her adolescence
trying to put his body in the path of lightning—

Doc says that's the only way to get back
to the future, the life you took for granted
before time became such a high-stakes game.

ST. ELMO'S FIRE (1985)

Near the nurses' station, Emilio Estevez asks
Andie MacDowell, "Do you still like Woody Allen
movies?" and the alarm system you've built
inside your body to track cultural offenses
goes off, but you're safe, Emilio Estevez
isn't in love with you; he didn't get a new job
just so he could stalk you in a chauffeured car,
or call the hospital where you work to find out
which ski resort you're at so he could drive
up there and humiliate himself before a stud
in a Pendleton blanket. *What is the tone*
of this movie, you might be asking yourself,
as Ally Sheedy's eyes brim with tears (again)—
the girl never takes off her pearls, not even
for shower sex. St. Elmo's fire is an electric
phenomenon that tricks sailors into thinking
they have to become Republicans to make
bank, when there are infinite other ways
to sell out. Rob Lowe's face demonstrates
the inverse relationship between sex appeal
and net worth in this universe—an empath

from a good family doesn't need a rich boyfriend;
she wants a lost boy, a reckless saxophonist
she can financially support until they negotiate
the terms and conditions of canceling her virginity.

CAN YOU MUTE YOURSELF DURING CORPSE POSE

Find your pelvis. Where did you last see it?
Externally rotate your anxiety until it points
at the ceiling. Maybe your face lifts, too.
Straighten both legs. Reverse warrior.
Slight back bend in trikonasana
like you're paying someone
to wash your hair in the beauty parlor
sink. Vinyasa or skip it.
Reach for your right foot
with your left hand and look
through the window of your armpit
at everything you haven't cleaned.
You can place your hands on blocks
or make a little pillow to cry into.
Eagle-wrap the arms. Open the hip.
If you can get your foot on your triceps,
you can float into dragonfly
or flash back to your last pedicure.
If you're not inverting, legs up the wall
is a great option for letting go

of your survival to-do list. Stay
for eight breaths and then we'll all meet
in savasana so no one's alone
in their final resting pose.

MEMORIAL DAY

Forgive me, distant wars, for bringing
flowers home.

—WISŁAWA SZYMBORSKA

Forgive me for not grasping the magnitude.
Forgive me for yesterday when I lay in the grass.
Forgive me, I could afford to stay safe.
I'm sorry it took me months to cry; I was so busy
coping, making dark jokes and performing
my identity: tough cookie. I'm trying to translate
this experience into an artifact that will mean
　　something
to readers of the future. I want them to know the era
our new normal was still *new*, how I wore my mask
to buy a pint of gelato because the season turned,
how I went outside and locked eyes with a robin
whose life is no worse without us. Forgive me
for I now understand the mindset of millionaires
following the news stories of the corrupt and inept,
the sick and the hungry, the hopeless, thinking,

But what can I, one person, do, while their small bubble

stays afloat on the current of good fortune.

Forgive me my gelato, this is a guilt poem.

Readers of the future, my apologies,

we were incapable of holding the whole catastrophe

in our heads, and so the paper of record printed

a meager accounting of the lives of the dead:

Helen Boles Days, 96, made what she had

work for her; Latasha Andrews, 33,

always the first to offer help

to those in need; Nita Pippins, 93, mother

to a generation of AIDS patients;

Melford Henson, 65, fell ill in prison

shortly before he was to be released.

I held the wall of names and turned

the pages with my inessential hands.

SIMULATION THEORY

Before all the gyms closed, I ran on the treadmill
and listened to a podcast about the likelihood

we're living in a sophisticated simulation,
one among many, our lives a research project

run by our own brilliant descendants
to find out how history might have turned

on different axes: *What if Hitler won*, etc.
You already know which *what if* we're in.

It would be dangerous to search for glitches
to prove the simulation is real,

says Preston Greene. Imagine a clinical trial,
if your subject figured out she's on the placebo.

You'd have to kill the trial.
We don't want researchers of the future

to annihilate our reality, but Preston,
what if that's what they're doing already?

The longer I live indoors, experiencing the outside
world through screens, the more plausible

the simulation theory seems.
It's somehow easier to imagine

a sadist in 2420 pushing a button
that says ADD PLAGUE and see what happens

to protest than it is to watch our demagogue
hold a Bible like a block of government cheese

and admit there's no master plan
other than to threaten more violence

against the people marching to stop
it. I'd like to speak to the manager

of this simulation. I'd like someone to tell me
how to prepare for what comes next.

WILD GEESE

after Mary Oliver

You do not have to be good
on Instagram so everyone sees.
You do not have to read
White Fragility on your knees
because it feels productive
to hurt. You do not have to
turn the Zoom meeting
into group therapy
about privilege
to prove you've done
the homework. Let your body
be anything other than a soft
animal to discipline and
groom. Let your body
be a body in motion
until your mind travels
beyond the territory

of your own despair.
The world goes on,
the wild geese keep crying
for us to look up from the page.

THE LIVES OF OTHERS (2006)

The playwright is one of the good ones
if by *good* we mean that he obeys
the dictates of the state to produce
art that celebrates the proletariat.
His beautiful girlfriend plays a factory
worker; made me think of Lucille Ball
on the assembly line (what an American
problem to have: you can't eat the candy
fast enough), except this is East Berlin
in 1984, no employment opportunities
for comediennes, but enough vodka
to take the edge off. In our imaginations,
we all would have played rebels
in the drama of history.
We'd know just where to hide
our contraband typewriter and how
to outsmart the Stasi. Harder to imagine
how we'd resist the pressure to conform
when we fail at this every day—
I'm speaking now to my comrades,
the artists, the ones who want to be seen

as good ones more than anything else.
Does the specter of surveillance
ever raise the hair on your neck
before you type what you think?
Have you considered which friend
you'd turn in if it allowed you to keep
working? Ulrich Mühe, who plays
HGW XX/7 in the film, performed *Hamlet*
in East Berlin because he felt theater
was the only place where the people
"weren't lied to," not realizing
he was being surveilled by four actors
and his wife, Jenny. When asked how
he prepared for his role as a Stasi captain,
he said, "I remembered."

ONE HUNDRED DAYS

> When worst got things, how was
> you? Steady on?
>
> —JOHN BERRYMAN

Time has taken on a peach-skin fuzz.
The rose-gold band of my tracking device

wears me. I count the nights I don't drink
because they distinguish my days.

We undertook a collective experiment
in sacrifice and obedience, but

at some point the trial
no longer seemed sustainable.

Tedium begs for a turning point.
It wasn't enough to be seen

on our best behavior. We wanted
to count for something

conspicuous, unmissable
even down for the count.

MUSEUM STUDIES

In the novel I'm reading, a woman
spends all day at the Met by herself
and my body said, *I remember.*

I've binged enough TV by now to miss
art that provokes a closer confrontation.
I haven't made eye contact with a portrait

in months. At the Louvre last October,
I took a picture of Brian taking a picture
of the *Mona Lisa* in a gallery crowded

with picture-takers, all replicating an original.
Going somewhere just to say I went there
isn't what I miss. It's the luxury of time

I had when I was young and my mind
was an autonomous zone, unregulated
by the tiny slot machine I keep touching

to see if this time I've won. Look
at me, Ms. Took It All for Granted,
the days I had to spend on art

I wasted, thinking there'd always be
more opportunities to see.
To be alone in public is a paradox

of privacy; you're the watcher
and the watched. To a tourist,
you're the American in headphones,

leather jacket, thrifted skirt, standing
in front of the water lily panorama,
making yourself the focal point.

The dead artists, how do we tell them
we now consume the world with cameras
turned on art and violence, ourselves?

THE KING OF STATEN ISLAND (2020)

Tried to think of the female equivalent of Judd Apatow
and couldn't. More opportunity for me, I guess.
Can you imagine a woman going to pitch
the inspired-by-true-events tale of a young man
who lives with his mom and smokes a lot of weed
to anesthetize his grief? I know this subject intimately,
if Hollywood would just give me two hours
and sixteen minutes to execute my vision.
My bona fides include the time I did an event
at a community college and a student told me
how much he related to the scene in my novel
where two guys play *Super Mario Kart*—
finally he saw his lived experience represented
in art. I remember what it was like to be twenty-two,
sitting on a couch, waiting for my real life
to start, just like the girls on Staten Island,
whose love language is impatience,
whose pity is corrupted affection.
They want to go dancing but no one
will acknowledge their bodies exist
beyond the walls of this basement

bong purgatory, who has any Xanax,
show her your tattoo, turn off the lights,
stop touching me with your feet,
put on a horror movie so the screams
of these idiots make us feel as high as kings.

HALO LIGHTING FOR AMATEURS

I wanted to look good enough to pass
as influential. I watched a YouTube tutorial
on what I could salvage from the crumbling
turn-of-the-century bungalow of a woman
I was: good bones, just needed some cosmetic
work, so I ordered $19 lipstick, a shade
called Anarchy (this was before the protests
inspired Soho storefronts to elevate
their plywood barricades with platitudes
to prevent the destruction of luxury).
Beauty brands are already forecasting
the future, a return to spending.
What's that shade you're wearing?
Oh, it's Dior's Defund the Po-po.
Who am I putting on perfume for?
Who will see my body below
my underwire? Remember how
we used to try on makeup in public,
back when it was safe to flirt
with dramatizing our appearance
one sanitized sample at a time?

ROMANTIC POET

When I drive to the specialty grocery store
that sells the parmesan without animal
rennet because now thou knowest too much
about how the cheese gets made, that's me
saying I love you. Bright star, I'm the minder
of our wedding budget spreadsheet,
supervisor of how much jargon
appears in thy work emails,
the scorekeeping scullery maid.
According to Keats, my love language
is "acts of service." I've memorized
your preferences so I can recite them
like lines written in early spring:
Have I not reason to lament
What man has made of man?
My friends call in peril
and I give them career advice—
when thou hast big hammer energy,
everything looketh like a nail. Four months
the length of five long winters,
I wandered lonely as a cloud and found

myself ending every phone call with
Love you, too. No one doubts my ability
to learn a new language. No one but you
sees the child I become at night,
after my shift is over, how adrift
I become over tasks undone.

EVERYWHERE YOU LOOK A SPECTACLE

I wake up and touch my phone to see
who was thinking of me as I slept.

Every day, a new series of betrayals
among the same players, Andy Samberg

in a Hawaiian print shirt, dinosaur spectator,
desert sunset, me in my bridesmaid dress

trying to suicide my way out of the time loop.
The subtweet is an art, like anything else.

I do it exceptionally well. I can cry on command
alongside the best of them. My touching, off-the-cuff

toast was perfected over the two decades
I spent scrolling past lonely avatars.

I would never say, *All you need is love*
but I might say, *Have you ever considered*

antidepressants? For our honeymoon,
we're going to 1994, where the notifications

arrive by mail. Anticipation is a turn-on
until your meet cute becomes routine.

Cristin Milioti had to teach herself
quantum physics on YouTube to escape

the rom-com's repetition glitch.
All I have to do is sign off,

all I have to do is sign off,
all I have to do is sign off.

THE LAST DANCE (2020)

Sing, O goddess, of the rage
that fueled the last Achilles
of the twentieth century; his name
was Michael Jordan and his *kleos*
was six hard-won championship trophies.
Whenever I bring up my love
for this series, my friends say,
"I heard he doesn't come across
as very nice," and I'm like, *Yeah, so?* When I die,
I hope my legacy is more compelling
than "She was nice and succeeded
in making everyone like her."
According to Gretchen Rubin's theory
of personality, Michael is an Upholder,
the rarest of tendencies
(Gretchen is, of course, herself one),
which means no one needs to tell MJ
to work out at 5 a.m. on game days, or to remake
his body for baseball, or how closely to clutch
his grievances, or to carry his team
on fumes when that's all he has left

in minute 44; his discipline is aspirational
to anyone who identifies as a Gretchen,
a compulsive overachiever; you might be one
if your sister texts you when she's on Adderall
to say she's turning into you, a monster
who knows trash-talking the competition
while practicing mindfulness is precisely
the kind of cognitive dissonance
Americans look for in a role model.
Be Like Mike, the hero of my epic
poem, set against the historic backdrop
of a sports dynasty, which, if you miss
The Bachelor, has everything:
all the high-stakes rivalry, sob stories, and
betrayals of your fave dating franchise,
not to mention men openly weeping
in each other's arms, intimacy
beyond Mike Fleiss's imagination.
I cried watching Scottie play through pain
in game six of the '98 finals, not only
when he touched the ball but when Michael
touched him, the ballet of collaborators
who don't need to speak when they think
in sync. (Pippen as Patroclus?)
Scottie undergoes Obliger-rebellion

according to Gretchen (speak, Muse!)
in episode 7, when he abruptly refuses
to play the final 1.8 seconds
in a game against the Knicks
because Phil Jackson wants Scottie
to pass to Kukoč. "Obliger-rebellion
may take a form that's small and symbolic,"
Gretchen says, or it "may be dramatic
and far-reaching, like abruptly quitting a job,
getting a divorce, or ending a long friendship,
with the feeling, 'I've had it. This is over.
You're dead to me.'" (Scottie apologized
in the locker room.) Even if you don't read
Gretchen's blog, you'll be able to identify
the team's rebel: Dennis Rodman,
whose performance mindset involves running away
to Las Vegas and marrying Carmen Electra;
I went through a motorcycle-riding period
in my life, too, I get it. I still carry a tiny rebel
around in my heart; she doesn't respond
well to supervision if she isn't given time off
to date Madonna and ride the open road.
When given the choice between laying siege
to Troy and achieving everlasting glory or
living a long life in suburban obscurity,

Michael issues a press release: "I'm back."
He never needed to change his hair color
for attention. He's too busy cataloging
his combatants' worst habits. The Trojans are losing
in Book XXII, and the shine on the armor of Achilles
blazes a way forward like the most brilliant star.

TRUTH OR CONSEQUENCES

On TV, a masked hospital physician
says half a million people went out to drink
the day after the bars reopened in L.A.,

like we paused the war to show off
our participation trophies.
I'm using the collective first person

because I'm not above desire
or the triggering effect that boredom
can have on the brain.

It is a truth universally acknowledged
that the more you have to drink,
the less you worry

about how much you had to drink.
Truth or Consequences, NM,
was put on the map for poets

to find, but a strip mall in Albuquerque
is where I completed my alcohol
server certification. A grad student

of American history played a VHS tape
of car wrecks and taught us which fatty foods
to serve those who insist on driving

home. Back then, reckless
was a costume I put on
when the occasion called.

I remember swimming in gin
because it was part of the obstacle course
laid out from one end of the night

to the other. The period of my life
when I was most likely to die
doing something ill-advised

I survived. This was years before the virus
turned alcohol into a conversation
about the economy instead

of admitting we want temporary oblivion,
a mini plague escape, pour me another paloma,
are we having fun yet, do you have anyone

you can call to take you home? In Albuquerque
drinking was how I manufactured enchantment
at each dead end in the labyrinth.

"I DON'T THINK I'M FAKE NEWS"

Florida became more flame-like.
I guess everybody makes mistakes.

I watch, I read. Look at the stuff.
I have a poll where we're leading

in every swing state. Joe doesn't know
he's alive. He doesn't even come out

of his basement. Let's take a test right now.
When you say "life," you mean abortion?

Count back from 100 by 7. We have embers
but we do have flames. I like a lot of liberal people.

Do you know how many times I've been written off?
Do you know we're not allowed to have a rally

in Michigan? They hate my guts. And it's a lie.
I heard we have the best mortality rate.

GROUNDHOG DAY (1993)

I'm a celebrity in an emergency:
I never had to care about other people
until I got stuck in a time loop where
all of a sudden there are consequences
for my behavior, and I'm beside myself.
I'll give you a hint, Phil, you're a dick
to work with, but it's the '90s,
when women were better at taking jokes
because they had no recourse
unless they wanted to be known
as the nagging-bitch-in-residence.
"I hate the term 'cancel culture,'"
Rita says in a winsome accent
as she lobs a snowball at a child.
"I prefer 'accountability culture.'"
"*Tu es très charmant,*"
the sardonic weatherman replies,
because he's had a thousand days
to become fluent in her love language.
Isn't it romantic when a marmot
brings a pockmarked misanthrope

and an upbeat lady together?
You couldn't make *Groundhog Day*
now because it's built on the premise
that even the most colossal jerk can learn
and grow—instead you'd have to make
a comedy where two hot cynics
drink themselves to death in the desert
because of quantum physics. Hilarious!
"What if there is no tomorrow?"
Phil asks, reading our minds
like a weather forecast.
"There wasn't one today."

VULNERABILITY HANGOVER

I admitted how I really felt
in an email newsletter.
Oopsie daisy! Is *cringe*
an onomatopoeia,
the sound my face
makes when I try
not to revisit
my best efforts
at "transparency,"
what everybody
allegedly "wants"?
Like my cyber sistren,
I made a career
sharing my feelings
in public. It's how I afford
therapy on my day off
from performing myself
for my Zoom audience.
What's everybody drinking
tonight, how do YOU practice
self care, whose idea was this

anyway, oh yeah mine,
forgot I'm living the dream.
My private self submits
anecdotes for my public
self's consideration, and as in any
overburdened bureaucracy,
the most deserving fall
through the cracks.
The next morning
I replay myself,
regretting what I didn't mask
behind a better joke,
how emotional I got
when I confessed
what I miss.

INSIDE MAN (2006)

Spike offered Denzel the role
of detective or criminal
mastermind, and Denzel
said he didn't want to rob
the bank—you can't act
with your face hidden
behind a mask.

HERETIC

God wanted to FaceTime and I declined.
I didn't want to have to explain millennials
to another boomer. We're going through
our dogma cycling phase. We rejected
hollow *thoughts and prayers* from the right,
but even Pelosi's *I pray for the president*
all the time sounds like an insult
cloaked by piety's pantsuit.
We want our own bespoke
spirituality, a direct-to-consumer
brand that figured out a way to disrupt
two thousand years of customer loyalty
to a single market leader.
We want a belief system
that can explain what makes us
so special, and we followed the feminist
astrologer's instructions to call the hospital
where we were born to ask *what time*
so we could claim an accurate star chart.
Nothing wrong with a quar hobby!
We were put here on earth to do *something*

to make money, so why not
build a brand around your rising sign?
If I sound cynical, please know
this is something I'm working on
by crying each time a person of faith
delivers a eulogy at one of the many
televised funerals this summer.
I cry whenever I hear people sing
in unison. I don't believe anyone
is irredeemable, which is something
I have in common with Jesus Christ,
but the new crusaders would eyeroll
emoji at my innocence before
scanning the horizon for the next skull
to bludgeon with their battle-ax.
If you don't believe in an afterlife
you must seek all your glory here on earth.

DER UNTERGANG (2004)

At the end, of course, everybody drank
while they waited to find out
if they'd die defending Berlin
from the Soviet advance or
find a good window
to commit suicide,
maybe with a friend,
what a way to go,
you light Eva Braun's cigarette
smile at the little Goebbels girls
finger your Iron Cross and
consider which of your drinking
buddies can be relied upon
to blow your brains out.
Der Führer might be the only sober one
in the bunker (our führer
doesn't drink either), and his last meal
is cheese ravioli, which is uncanny
only if you identify as vegetarian.
The most sympathetic character
is the secretary whose downfall

is her own curiosity, a familiar
story in Western civilization—
even she questions whether youth
is any excuse for devotion.
All the Nazis in this DIY death camp
are painted pathetic, desperate, and
hopeless, unlike Scorsese's
or Tarantino's antiheroes, the charismatic
avengers, comedic criminals, and
femme fatales you'd never see
kill six kids on camera. Only people
who have reckoned with their history
could make a film so unflattering,
so senseless in eleventh-hour violence,
the potential for glory zilch. In America
we're too committed to exceptionalism
to admit we're losing this war,
as the nightly news reports the death tally,
and we send our children back to school
so they can learn to read and write
the story—someday—of our failure.

WHEN AM I

Time flies when you're pressed for time.
I can donate money, but I can't time-share
with my friend who doesn't have enough
hours for childcare and the life of the mind
that keeps her lights on. *Better late than never*
is what the talking heads will tell us
when there's an effective vaccine.
Aller droit au but, as they say in France,
but their president doesn't have the IQ
of an oyster. Time for an election.
Time to sign off. No one likes to hear
their time at the mic has expired.
Il est temps de tourner la page.
Everyone's trying to beat the clock,
but no one can tell me if it's Tuesday.

ARGUMENTUM AD MISERICORDIAM

Miss Americana doesn't ask how many posters
she has to sign before she can go to bed,
whether she can rock the bodysuit
without looking like a Queen Bey knock-off,
or how the boomers in the room benefit
each time she asks permission
before expressing an opinion in public.
She tried too hard to be perfect is the narrative
critics are calling "raw" and "revealing"
in the doc that debuted at Sundance, but
I assume her team workshopped which
of her vulnerabilities to expose
in order to be maximally relatable
to white girls who aren't believed
when they say their pain is real. Starving
for attention and denying yourself
the pleasure of a burrito for years
are familiar tropes; so is divulging
the most dreadful thing
that's been done to you.
(I never see starlets confessing

the worst sin they've committed
against someone else.)
Taylor is no rebel. She's a Gretchen,
an Upholder, who hasn't yet liberated
herself from the costume carousel
of Miss Fill-in-the-Blank.

EXPERIENCE ECONOMY

It's not over if you can afford to pay
to find out if you're infected
before you party; *my healthcare concierge*
told me I didn't need a mask tonight
is the future of the Real Housewives
franchise. They removed the velvet ropes
from night clubs and said, *Education*
is exclusive now, and the same white people
who spent the summer studying abroad
on Black Instagram learning to speak
privilege were eager to spend theirs
hiring the most racially diverse MIT grad
they could find in this competitive market,
plus a crew of *como se dice* manual laborers
to put up the $30,000 prefab shed where
their children could have a shot at normal
brain development, too late for me
I've already spent so much of my life on screens
I've destroyed my attention span

for listening to rich women
tell me they had no choice
but to pay for the best.

THE REAL

Everything I know about female friendship
I learned from shows with "the real" in the title:

how to confront someone who's stolen your brand,
how to cause a scene while writing a book

on manners, how to discuss your husband's suicide
on camera. I don't have boundaries

as much as I have bridges I have lit
and turned away from as they burned,

preferring ultimate ruin to confrontation
like the kidnapping of Helen becomes moot

when there's a war that needs its soldiers.
The real problem is my pattern

of falling in love with women who say
I'm all they've got and then failing

to achieve my purpose of serving
as their universe. For the season finale,

I wore a flamingo costume (long story)
and was too conspicuous to miss,

nursing my piña colada while I inventoried
the loves of my life, all the girls whose beds

I'd slept in when they threatened harm
and how we called each other sister

until our family was just like any other—wrecked
by different interpretations of a single wound.

LINCOLN, ABRAHAM, MELANCHOLY OF

He had a Sad Nature, many said
of Lincoln, or as Emily put it,
It feels a shame to be Alive—
when Men so brave—are dead—
dashing off a war that was no metaphor
& she would appreciate a last-chance
candidate who wears Grief as his mantle
& can quote poetry by heart,
which I admit softened the cynic
who patrols the border inside me
to prevent any Hope from crossing.
For four nights we watched footage
of losses: a father lost his job,
a husband lost his wife & daughter
& then his son, which reminded me
of Lincoln—how he went to Willie's tomb
when he yearned once more to hold him.
Did you ever dream of a lost friend
& feel that you were having a direct communion
with that friend & yet a consciousness

that it was not a reality? he asked the army officer

guarding the mausoleum. The man answered

yes—the year was 1862 & the whole country

waded Grief, whole Pools of it. Our last-chance

candidate is running on empathy

in a contest between *It is what it is* &

the parable Lincoln loved to tell

of the ancient king who wanted a proverb

that would apply at all times,

in every situation. His wise men said,

And this, too, shall pass away.

FRAMING DEVICE

Day six, 'tis Filomena's turn to play
queen, and she tells of a knight

who offers a lady a horseback ride
in the form of one of the finest stories

in the world, but he is no better master
of his weapon than of his story, and

he tells it so ill she prays him
to dismount her. I recognize

the face of a woman listening
to a man rehearse his greatest hits

until he strikes a chord in tune
as my own. 'Twas just the other night—

the weather as fine as it was, I searched
"outdoor dining" and went on foot

to a tavern, where I met a knight
who wanted to give me a ride

on what his life had become: working
to build enough cottages to satisfy

the market demands of millionaires
in a town where the school mascot

is the Monopoly man. Barzun says decadent
society is marked by a peculiar restlessness,

the search in every direction for a new faith.
All my life I have worn this listening face

turned up at men who never got the sympathy
bouquets they deserved and at women

who keep meticulous accounts
of who wronged them, how, and when.

Like the knight, we don't wait
to understand the narrative

before we begin our recitation.
In the attention economy,

there's no incentive for reticence
like there is for laughing wild

amid severest woe.
I am writing in the vernacular

of this *annus horribilis*
to dispel the melancholy

of the ladies. Some will say I took too much
license in writing these stories, that

I didn't suffer like my peers to perform
the correct politics, at a time

when it was acceptable for even the most virtuous
to go about with their breeches on their heads

if they thought it would preserve their lives,
Boccaccio concludes in self-defense.

Ladies, ladies, ladies, ladies,
for whose solace I addressed myself,

may they say about the ride I gave,
that at least I made some mischief.

ACKNOWLEDGMENTS

Chelsea Hodson's early encouragement of these poems was critical (she also gets credit for discovering the book's title!). My literary agent, Erin Hosier, recognized that I was writing a book before I did—thank you, Erin, for championing my work and looking out for my sanity whenever I get *too online*. Editing poetry is a delicate art and I have been so fortunate to work with Sarah Lyn Rogers on this collection. Sarah, you have an exceptional gift; thank you for sharing it with me. To my friends who let me talk about Twitter so much, and who gently remind me there is more to life than working, thank you: Brittany Allen, Grace Do, Claire Dunnington, Liz Hildreth, Lily Ladewig, Julia Phillips, Kat Rosenfield, Alizah Salario, Sharon Shula, Julia Strayer, and Elizabeth Trundle. Thank you, Doree Shafrir and Kate Spencer, for having me on the *Here for You* pod, and to Rob MacDonald for publishing my poem "Heretic" in *Sixth Finch*. Lastly, I want to thank Rob, Jason Koo, and Ricardo Maldonado for supporting my poetry, even during the long fallow period when I wasn't writing any.

NOTES

I used Wayne Rebhorn's translation of *The Decameron* (Norton Critical Editions) and J. M. Rigg's 1903 translation on Brown University's *Decameron Web* project.

"Think Starlight": the metaphor comes from a March 13 story about COVID-19 in *The New York Times*. Dr. Carter Mecher, an adviser for public health at the Department of Veterans Affairs, told the *Times*: "By the time you have a death in the community, you have a lot of cases already. It's giving you insight into where the epidemic was, not where it is. Think starlight. That light isn't from now, it's from however long it took to get here."

"Catastrophe Tourism" references an excerpt from Mark O'Connell's book *Notes from an Apocalypse*, published in *The New York Times Magazine* on March 24, 2020. In 1944, before the Red Cross visited Theresienstadt, 7,503 Jews were deported to Auschwitz, to make the "spa town" hoax believable. Some of the children's opera *Brundibár* was filmed for propaganda. After the last performance, the children were put onto cattle cars.

Of the fifteen thousand children at Theresienstadt, only one hundred survived.

"Outside Time": Writer/director Madeleine Olnek made the film *Wild Nights with Emily* after learning about the research Martha Nell Smith, a Dickinson scholar, had done to uncover the erasure of the name Susan from Emily's letters. (Susan Huntington Gilbert was Emily's childhood friend and, upon marrying Austin Dickinson, became her sister-in-law.)

"*Tiger King* (2020)": Lorrie Moore wrote about Trump's voice in an essay published in *The New Yorker* on April 6, 2020. The Moore short story referenced in this poem is "Debarking."

"Memorial Day": On May 24, 2020, the entire front page of *The New York Times* was a list of people who lost their lives to Coronavirus, as the death toll in America reached 100,000.

"Simulation Theory": The podcast is Robert Wright's interview of Preston Greene for MeaningofLife.tv on November 1, 2019.

"*The Last Dance* (2020)": You can take a quiz on Gretchen Rubin's website to find out which tendency you have.

"'I Don't Think I'm Fake News'" is a found poem based on the Chris Wallace interview with Donald Trump on July 19, 2020.

"Lincoln, Abraham, Melancholy Of": I drew inspiration from Joshua Wolf Shenk's book *Lincoln's Melancholy*. The lines "It feels a shame to be Alive— / when Men so brave—are dead—" and "I can wade Grief— / Whole Pools of it" are Emily Dickinson's.

LEIGH STEIN is the author of five books, including the novel *Self Care* and the poetry collection *Dispatch from the Future*. She has also written for *The New York Times*, *The Washington Post*, *Allure*, *Elle*, *The Cut*, *Salon*, and *Slate*. She is a recipient of an Amy Award from *Poets & Writers*, and *The Cut* named her "poet laureate of *The Bachelor*."